Nightlife Queen
—— to ——
Kingdom Queen

Escaping the Darkness and
Embracing the Light

KOURTNEY "KP" PINA

Nightlife Queen to Kingdom Queen
Escaping the Darkness and Embracing the Light
Copyright © 2025 Kourtney 'KP' Pina

For permission requests, contact: Purpose Publishing via email at contactus@purposepublishing.com.

For speaking engagements, interviews, bulk orders, or promotions contact the author via email at kourtneypina@gmail.com and stay connected at www.KourtneyPina.com

Printed in the United States of America

Paperback ISBN - 978-1-965319-52-9
eBook ISBN- 978-1-965319-53-6

Purpose Publishing LLC.

13194 US Highway 301 South, Suite 417
Riverview, Florida 33578

www.PurposePublishing.com

Dedication

A Letter to My Father ...

I dedicate this book to the ministry God birthed through my surrender—
This book is for the altar You built from my ashes.

To the Kingdom assignment that called me out of darkness—
I am returning to you the platform I once built for my own name.
Now it belongs to you, Lord, and you alone.

To every woman I will serve, mentor, and lead—
May this be your mirror, your map, your moment of awakening.

*And to the **Kingdom Queen,** whom I was always positioned to be—*
Even when I was lost, You never revoked my crown.
Even when I rebelled, You preserved my place.
You called me daughter when I didn't feel worthy to be called a servant.

I dedicate this to the purpose You wrote before the world began.
*This book is the evidence that Your **grace wins**, **obedience breaks chains**,*
*and **identity in Christ reigns**.*

This is for Your glory.
Forever and only—Yours.

Chapter Outline

1. The Seduction of Success 1

2. Queen of the Night, Slave to the Darkness 9

3. The Voice in the Silence 17

4. When God Called, I Ran Toward the Light 25

5. Notebooks of Heaven 33

6. Deliverance in the Secret Place 41

7. The Word That Found Me 49

8. Beauty for Ashes 57

9. The Other Side of Obedience 65

10. Queen Reborn 73

Epilogue: To the Queen Still in the Dark 81

Chapter 1

The Seduction of Success

I was thirty-five and walking through the doors of my own empire.

The floor of Lit Cigar & Martini Lounge shimmered under the glow of soft lighting. Music danced in the air, top-shelf bottles lined custom-built shelves like luxury soldiers, and the scent of power, money, and desire clung to everything. Cameras flashed, laughter filled the air, celebrities lounged in our plush booths, and I? I was the queen. People didn't just want to come to the club—they wanted to *be* me.

It was 2021. Tampa had just awakened from the heavy slumber of the pandemic. While the world reeled from loss and uncertainty, we became a lighthouse of liberation. People rushed out of isolation and into our doors, desperate to remember what it felt like to live, to indulge, to forget. And there I stood in the middle of it all—successful, admired, envied, applauded. The money flowed. The status soared. We were nominated as one of Tampa's Top 3 Small Businesses of the Year.

Yet the deeper I climbed into the spotlight, the further my soul descended into silence.

You see, no one tells you how dark success can be when it's birthed without God. No one warns you that the same crown that makes

1

you feel powerful can also slowly kill you. No one tells you that attention is addictive—and once it has you, it will never let you rest. You become what people expect. When the world applauds, you don't stop to ask if God approves.

I didn't realize it then, but I was being seduced—not by a man, not by a product, not even by fame. I was being seduced by the spirit of this world. The spirit that promises influence, wealth, favor, and attention but hides the fine print: exhaustion, anxiety, betrayal, spiritual blindness, and isolation. I signed the contract with my own ambition. Success became my god, and I worshiped at its altar.

I gave it my body, my nights, my friendships, my identity. I poured everything I had into being seen, needed, adored, and feared. As a result, the world rewarded me with followers, headlines, invitations, and access, but I was spiritually bankrupt. I didn't realize the lie I was living. I didn't know I had become both queen and prisoner of the very empire I built.

But God did.

The truth is, you don't have to be evil to be lost. Sometimes, all it takes is to be *busy*—too busy for stillness, too driven to ask questions, too successful to notice you've never actually had peace.

Let me say this to you, women reading these words: ***Just because the world is clapping, doesn't mean Heaven is.***

In the world's eyes, I had everything. Yet in the spirit, I had nothing. I wore crowns made of applause. I dressed my wounds in designer labels. I hid my fear behind filters and my depression behind events. Though people constantly surrounded me, I'd come home at night, remove my lashes, my heels, my smile—I didn't know who I was anymore.

Have you ever reached the top of the mountain only to realize it was the wrong mountain?

This is not a chapter about regret. It's about realization. That realization is what set me on a journey of rescue I didn't know I needed.

Because here's the truth: *Success without surrender is seduction.* The enemy loves nothing more than a woman who is adored by the world but disconnected from her Creator.

Maybe you're reading this in your own version of Lit Lounge. Maybe your throne looks different—an office, a relationship, a platform, a career, a lifestyle that others worship but you secretly hate. Perhaps you, too, are applauded but spiritually suffocating.

Let me gently ask you this: *What are you trading for applause?*

Because one day, I stood in a room full of admirers and felt completely alone. That's when I heard the whisper—not from a person, not from a podcast, but from deep within:

"Daughter, there is more."

I didn't know it then, but God was about to shake my entire life. Not to punish me—but to rescue me. Because when God loves you, He will interrupt your delusion. He will disturb your false peace. He will dismantle your false crown. Not because He wants to see you fall—but because He knows what He placed inside you is too sacred to stay in the dark.

So began the shaking.

However, before I reveal how I escaped the darkness, I must tell you that even darkness has charm. It's not always evil-looking. It's seductive. Beautiful. Sparkling. That's why many don't know they're in it until it's choking them.

I was admired, envied, celebrated—but I was in chains.

Chains made of gold.

Chains that looked like success.

Chains that nearly cost me my soul.

Now that I've been rescued, and I've walked away from the kingdom of night and into the Kingdom of Light, I will spend every word of this book showing you the way out. Not just out of the club. Not just out of the lifestyle. But out of *any lie* that has kept you from your true identity in Christ.

Because I'm not just telling you my story. I'm handing you the keys to your freedom.

You are not forgotten. You are not too far gone. You are not too dirty, too broken, too famous, too ashamed.

You are seen. You are wanted. You are royal.

But first, you must trade the world's crown for God's. You must lay down your throne to receive His. Because the seduction of success may be loud, but the voice of God? It will save your life.

He's whispering even now. Are you listening?

Scripture Meditation:

"What good is it for someone to gain the whole world, yet forfeit their soul?"—Mark 8:36

Queen's Challenge:

Find a quiet space today. Sit without music, without distractions. Ask yourself honestly:

♛ What have I been chasing?

_____

_____

_____

_____

_____

_____

♛ Is it from God or from the world?

_____

_____

_____

_____

_____

♛ What am I gaining on the outside but losing on the inside?

_____

_____

_____

_____

_____

_____

Journal your answers. Then ask God this simple prayer:

"Lord, show me what I've been calling success that You call slavery."

How does the scripture speak to your heart?

_____

_____

_____

_____

_____

_____

_____

_____

_____

_____

_____

_____

_____

_____

_____

_____

_____

_____

_____

NIGHTLIFE QUEEN TO KINGDOM QUEEN

_____

_____

_____

_____

_____

_____

_____

_____

_____

_____

_____

_____

_____

_____

_____

_____

_____

_____

_____

_____

_____

_____

_____

_____

Chapter 2

Queen of the Night, Slave to the Darkness

They called me powerful.

They called me inspiring, magnetic, untouchable. They said I was the one who "made it," the woman who defied the odds, who built a brand from scratch and stood at the top while others scrambled below. In public, I was royalty. I was someone whom everyone wanted to know. And in the kingdom of nightlife, I reigned supreme.

Yet behind the scenes, I was unraveling.

At first, I didn't even recognize it. The breakdown doesn't always look like a dramatic collapse; it often comes like a slow leak—one little compromise, one more late night, one more business deal that costs more than money. The pressure builds quietly. The cracks form under luxury tiles, and the weight of pretending becomes unbearable.

Inside the four walls of my club, I curated perfection. The lighting was flawless, the music smooth, the cocktails divine. But in my soul, it was chaos. I was managing appearances while internally hemorrhaging. I was simultaneously the architect and the prisoner of what I had built.

There is a unique kind of torment that comes when you are celebrated outwardly and tormented inwardly. I could not escape the duality—Queen of the Night on the outside, slave to the darkness on the inside.

The truth is, the deeper I went into the empire I was building, the further I was from the woman God had designed me to be. The very crown I wore in public was forged in private compromise.

I trusted people I shouldn't have. I ignored the red flags because the money was good. I allowed flattery to cover manipulation.

Eventually, the inner circle—those closest to me—became the greatest threat to my peace. The business partners I once considered brothers and sisters started to shift. Their energy changed. Their eyes watched me with suspicion, not support. The deeper my influence grew, the more their loyalty thinned. I felt it, like a chill in a once warm room.

Jealousy is a silent killer. In the world of performance and profit, loyalty is often temporary. However, the betrayal that hurt the most didn't come from them. It came from me.

I had betrayed myself. I had silenced the small voice inside that warned me early on. I had convinced myself I could manage it, manipulate it, maneuver around it. I had made myself a god in my own world. Now, the weight of my crown was choking me.

The enemy works like this: He never demands everything up front. He asks for one compromise, one silence, one agreement at a time. Then, before you know it, you've surrendered your soul one decision at a time. You're dressed like a queen but living in chains. You speak of power, but feel powerless. You smile, but cry on the floor when the guests leave.

Maybe you know what I mean.

Maybe you've built a brand, a life, a reputation, a family—and deep down, you know it's all too fragile. Too empty. Too loud. Too fake.

Perhaps you, like I was, are exhausted from pretending to be okay.

Let me offer you something I wish someone had told me then: *just because everyone wants your life doesn't mean it's a life worth living.*

Fame without peace is torment. Success without surrender is idolatry, and favor from the world means nothing if you are falling apart in secret.

I remember one night vividly. It was a sold-out event featuring a live performance with an artist. I wore a beautiful dress, greeted the celebrities, and posed for every camera. Still, I remember slipping into the bathroom, locking the stall, and thinking, *Why am I here?* There was no visible reason. I realized I truly hated it. I was in so much pain. Emptiness. I felt so trapped with a deep ache of knowing I didn't belong—yet found myself powerless to escape.

That night, I looked at myself in the mirror and whispered, "I can't keep doing this."

I wasn't talking about the club. I was talking about "the life."

The performance. The pretending. The slow dying inside of a woman who had given the world everything and now had nothing left to give herself.

This chapter isn't about shame. It's about revelation. God began awakening me gently. The Holy Spirit didn't come to condemn me—He came to pull me from the fire.

Sometimes, the first sign of your rescue is your breakdown. Because when you're finally too tired to pretend, you've created space for truth to speak.

God had not forgotten me. He was watching the whole time—waiting.

Now, He was whispering in the darkness: *Daughter, you were never meant to wear that crown. I have a different one for you.*

I didn't know it yet, but this was the beginning of deliverance. Not just from the club. Not just from the partners. Not just from the lifestyle, but from myself.

Because the scariest prison is the one you decorate so beautifully, you forget it's a cell. Now I could see the bars, and I wanted out.

Maybe this is where you are, too. Perhaps you've dressed your prison in designer labels, accolades, degrees, titles, or followers. But late at night, when it's just you and God, something aches. Something groans. Something inside whispers, "*There has to be more.*"

You're not wrong—there *is* more. However, first, you have to admit that you're not free.

Only then can the journey to the Kingdom begin.

Only then can the light break through.

Only then can the real crown—the eternal one—be revealed.

It starts with surrender, and surrender starts here.

Scripture Meditation:

"Woe to those who call evil good and good evil, who put darkness for light and light for darkness."—Isaiah 5:20

Queen's Challenge:

Ask yourself:

♛ Where am I pretending to be powerful, but in honesty, feel powerless?

_____

_____

_____

_____

_____

_____

♛ What crowns have I accepted that God never gave me?

_____

_____

_____

_____

_____

♛ Where have I silenced His voice in favor of applause?

_____

_____

_____

_____

_____

_____

Write down what God reveals. Then ask Him this simple but life-changing question:

"God, show me what I've built in darkness so I can walk in Your light."

How does the scripture speak to your heart?

_____

_____

_____

_____

_____

_____

_____

_____

_____

_____

_____

_____

_____

_____

_____

_____

_____

_____

NIGHTLIFE QUEEN TO KINGDOM QUEEN

Chapter 3

The Voice in the Silence

Silence is terrifying when you've lived your life in noise.

I had mastered the art of noise—music vibrating from floor to ceiling, heels clacking across the shiny epoxy floors, money being made over laughter and liquor, applause echoing through sold-out events. Silence, to me, had always signaled absence—an absence of people, power, and relevance. In the nightlife, silence was something to run from. Fill it. Drown it. Control it.

Yet when the applause fades and the lights shut down, you're left alone with yourself. In that quiet, a different voice begins to speak.

It wasn't long after that breaking point in the bathroom mirror that I started to notice the silence more. It wasn't just around me—it was inside me. A stillness that felt foreign at first. Instead of filling it with noise again, something in me said, *Wait. Just listen.*

One night, after yet another event left me feeling more drained than celebrated, I came home, sat in the middle of my office floor still in full glam, and I cried out to the Holy Spirit something I hadn't said in years:

"God, are You there? If you are real, please save me. I'm dying here."

It wasn't dramatic. There was no choir. No vision. No angelic visitation.

Just silence, but this silence was different.

It wasn't empty—it was holy.

Suddenly, something happened that I didn't expect. I started to cry—not because of sadness, but because I *felt* Him. I felt a presence in the room that was more real than anything I had experienced in a long time. Not just emotional relief. Not just release. Presence.

He didn't shout. He whispered. Yet His whisper thundered through every part of me that had been numb.

The world had screamed for years: *Be more. Do more. Look the part. Own the room.*

Yet God whispered: *I am real, I have been waiting for you, and you don't have to perform anymore. Just be Mine.*

That moment became a threshold—a holy interruption. A gentle but unshakable knowing that the life I was living was no longer sustainable, and that He was offering me another way—a way out.

If you're reading this, maybe you know exactly what I'm talking about. Perhaps you're just now hearing the whisper.

Maybe you're starting to feel something stirring inside you that's hard to explain—an ache for more, a knowing that something needs to change. That voice you hear in the silence? That quiet conviction? That holy discomfort?

That's Him. That's God.

The world will tell you to run from silence. To fill it. To numb it. In truth, silence is where God speaks. It is the sacred chamber where the lies fall quiet and truth has room to breathe.

I didn't become radically changed overnight. Though that moment—sitting on the floor in makeup and complete brokenness—was the first true prayer I'd prayed in years. It wasn't eloquent. It wasn't even confident. It was more like desperation.

It was honest, and that's all God needed.

For the first time, I didn't ask for a blessing. I asked for a rescue. I wasn't seeking a promotion. I was seeking peace. Although I didn't know it, that one whisper of surrender opened a door to everything that would follow.

You see, God doesn't shout to compete with the noise. He waits until you're ready to listen. The moment I quieted the voices of culture, expectation, and ego—even briefly—I heard the whisper of my Father.

That voice did not shame me. It didn't list my failures or remind me of all I'd done wrong.

It said, *You are still Mine, and I am still here.*

Tears rolled down my cheeks as a thought settled over me like warm oil: *God, you never left. You were the only one who never left me.*

Every night I stood smiling but secretly empty, He was there. Every time I trusted the wrong person, He saw.

Every time I traded intimacy with Him for approval from others, He waited.

God was never far. I was just too loud and distracted to hear Him.

Yet, in the silence, I heard Him clearly—not with my ears, but with my spirit.

Let me tell you something I learned that night and have held onto ever since: *God's silence is never His absence.*

Sometimes He's silent because He's waiting for you to stop running.

Sometimes He's silent because He wants to see if you'll choose Him without a spectacle.

Sometimes He's silent so you'll finally come to the end of yourself— and make room for Him to begin.

I want to speak directly to the woman reading this who feels numb, tired, and far from God: You don't need to pray the perfect prayer. You don't need a theology degree. You don't need to clean up your act before you come.

You merely need to say His name.

He will meet you in your car. In your bathroom. In your mess. In your silence—just like He did for me.

You may not hear an audible voice, but trust me—when God speaks, you *know*. He speaks in peace. He speaks with clarity. He speaks in presence. His voice is forever tethered to love.

If you feel that stirring, don't run. Lean in. Turn everything off, and whisper, *"God, is that you? Are You there?"*

He will answer—He's already speaking.

The question is, are you listening?

> **Scripture Meditation:**
>
> *"And after the fire came a gentle whisper."*—1 Kings 19:12

Queen's Challenge:

Create a space of silence this week. No distractions. No scrolling. No background noise. Just you and God.

Then ask:

- ♛ What is God trying to say in my silence?

  _____

  _____

  _____

  _____

  _____

  _____

- ♛ What have I been too loud to hear?

  _____

  _____

  _____

  _____

  _____

  _____

  _____

Journal what you feel. Don't rush it. Even five minutes can change everything.

Prayer:

"Lord, I'm listening. Speak to me. Whisper truth where lies once lived. Show me You're near."

How does the scripture speak to your heart?

_____

_____

_____

_____

_____

_____

_____

_____

_____

_____

_____

_____

_____

_____

_____

_____

_____

NIGHTLIFE QUEEN TO KINGDOM QUEEN

Chapter 4

When God Called, I Ran
Toward the Light

There is a moment in every woman's story—if she listens close enough—when the whisper turns into a call.

Not just a nudge. Not just a stirring. A *call*.

A divine summons from the depths of Heaven that says, *Come out from where you are. It's time.*

For me, that moment didn't come with flashing lights or dramatic visions. It came with an *ache* I could no longer ignore.

After I sat in that sacred silence and whispered, "God, are You there?" something inside me shifted. It was as if a veil had been lifted. I could still hear the music from the club, still see the faces of my partners and patrons, still feel the weight of the world I had built—but now it all felt … *empty*. It didn't sparkle the way it used to. It didn't satisfy. The glamour didn't grip me anymore.

I had tasted the beginning of God's presence, and now I couldn't go back to anything less.

What followed was not some overnight spiritual makeover. It was messy. It was raw. But it was *real*. I started craving something I had never truly desired before—*truth*. Not performance. Not appearance. Not applause.

God. His Word. His voice. His truth.

I found myself waking up early—not for business calls, not to check revenue—but to read the Bible and to pray. I don't mean casually scrolling through a verse on a pretty app: I mean digging, studying, cross-referencing, watching sermons, and listening to teachings late into the night. I devoured the scripture like I was starving. Honestly? I was.

I was spiritually malnourished. I had feasted on affirmation and aesthetics for so long that I didn't realize how sick my soul had become.

However, the moment I tasted God's Word—really tasted it—I became addicted.

It was like water in the desert. Like light in a cave. Like oxygen in a room I hadn't realized was suffocating me.

The more I studied, the more I began to see Him—not just in the Bible, but in my life. He was there when the doors opened at Lit Cigar & Martini Lounge. He was there when the betrayal came. He was there in my moments of compromise. Not approving but patiently waiting. *Calling.*

And now, I was answering.

The more I pursued Him, the more He revealed Himself. Not just as Savior—but as Father. As Counselor. As Lover of my soul. And the intimacy? It was indescribable. It wasn't about religion. It wasn't about rules. It was about the relationship.

God wasn't demanding I fix everything overnight. He was only saying, "Walk with Me." So, I did.

I started turning down events. Declining invites. Pulling back from partnerships that didn't align with what I was learning. At first, people were confused. Some mocked. Others whispered behind my back. I felt like I was being attacked.

Still, I didn't care.

For the first time, I wasn't following people—I was following Jesus. I wasn't living for people—I was living for Jesus, and He was leading me somewhere *better*.

I would wake up in tears some mornings—not out of pain, but out of *awe*. How had I missed this? How had I lived so long surrounded by fame and still never felt this full?

I was falling in love. Deeply. Eternally. With the One who loved me before I ever said His name.

I remember journaling late into the night, writing scriptures over and over again like they were medicine—because they were. I wasn't reading to perform or to be spiritual. I was reading because the truth was setting me free, verse by verse, line by line.

The hunger for God became the most beautiful obsession I've ever known.

I started noticing changes. Not just in how I dressed or how I talked—but how I thought. My desires shifted. My ambitions changed. What I used to crave became repulsive to me. What I used to idolize became insignificant. I had no desire for the throne of culture anymore.

I wanted the **Kingdom**.

Let me be clear: God didn't rip me from the nightlife—*I walked out.* Because once you've tasted real light, the darkness loses its charm.

I don't know who this chapter is for, but if you feel that hunger rising in you—don't ignore it. *That hunger is Holy.* That thirst is your soul recognizing the voice of its Creator. Choose Him.

You don't need to understand it all right now—you only need to say yes.

God will meet you where you are. In the mess. In the confusion. In the contradiction. He's not asking for perfection. He's asking for your heart.

And when you give it to Him—really give it—He'll take you places no club, no career, no relationship, no accolade ever could.

Places of peace.

Places of purpose.

Places of power—not the kind that crushes others, but that sets people free.

When God called me, I ran toward the light. And every step I've taken since has been proof that when you walk toward Him, *He runs toward you.*

So to the woman reading this who feels the pull—you feel that gentle tug in your spirit—you're not crazy. I promise!

You're being called.

So run. Run as fast as you can.

You won't regret it. I promise. He promises.

> **Scripture Meditation:**
>
> "You will seek Me and find Me when you seek Me with all your heart."—Jeremiah 29:13

Queen's Challenge:

Begin your pursuit of God today. Choose one gospel (Matthew, Mark, Luke, or John) and commit to reading one chapter a day.

Prayer:

"God, make me hungry for You. Speak to me through Your Word. Show me who You are—and who I am in You."

Then journal what He shows you. Don't overthink it. Just start.

Because obedience begins with one small step toward the light.

How does the scripture speak to your heart?

NIGHTLIFE QUEEN TO KINGDOM QUEEN

Chapter 5

Notebooks of Heaven

There are moments in the Christian journey that feel like fire—undeniable, immediate, consuming. Then some seasons feel more like construction: quiet, meticulous, intimate. Not flashy, but foundational.

That was this season for me.

After I responded to God's call and began devouring His Word, something awakened inside me that had been dormant all along—a student's heart. Not of business. Not of branding. But of truth. I wasn't just reading the Bible. I was *studying it*—and more than that, I was meeting God inside it.

It began with a single scripture.

I remember reading it, then reading it again, and realizing that one line held *more life* than any book, quote, or motivational speech I had ever heard. That single scripture became a mirror. It showed me my wounds. It showed me my identity. It showed me the faithfulness of the One who had never stopped pursuing me.

So I picked up a notebook—just one at first. I didn't know it would become a sacred habit.

That notebook became my altar. My sanctuary. My battlefield and my balm. Scripture after scripture, I copied them down. Word for word. Line after line. Sermons would lead me to new verses, verses would lead me to questions, and the Holy Spirit would lead me to revelation.

I began to understand who I was—not because a motivational quote said so, but because God Himself said so. Through scripture, I was learning the language of the Kingdom. Once you understand it, the language of the world no longer satisfies.

Let me say this clearly: The Word of God is not just a book. It's a voice. It's a presence. It's a weapon.

Every scripture I wrote became a brick in the foundation of my new life. It wasn't always emotional. Some mornings I read without tears. Some nights I studied while still battling old habits. But I never stopped writing. Never stopped seeking.

Because I wasn't just learning—I was being transformed. My mind was being renewed.

This process was holy. Private. Sometimes slow, but always supernatural.

Here's what I began to notice:

- ♚ My thoughts were changing.

- ♚ My conversations were changing.

- ♚ My confidence was changing.

- ♚ My discernment was deepening.

- ♚ My hunger was increasing.

This wasn't behavior modification. It was identity restoration.

I was no longer just trying to be a "better person." I was becoming a new creation—a Kingdom woman.

Every lie the world had taught me—about my body, my worth, my role, my voice—was being dismantled by truth. And the more I let the Word in, the more the old me had to go.

If I could reach back and tell my younger self anything, I'd say this: "You're not broken. You're just unrooted. Plant yourself in the Word, and you will grow into everything God created you to be."

I say that now to you, too.

To the woman reading this who feels confused, distant from God, overwhelmed by life: You don't need another social media reel. You don't need another feel-good quote.

You need the Word.

If you want peace, open your Bible.

If you want purpose, open your Bible.

If you want power, open your Bible.

Start small. One verse. One chapter. One notebook.

Let God meet you there. He is not hiding. He has been waiting.

If you're wondering where to begin, begin with the Gospels. Start with Jesus. Look at how He spoke to women. Watch how He saw the unseen. Study how He moved in both tenderness and authority.

Then write it down. Record what pierces you. Write what convicts you.

Keep your own *Notebook of Heaven*.

Then one day, you'll look back and realize those pages aren't just filled with ink and scripture. They are filled with evidence of your deliverance because this is how transformation happens: one Word at a time.

Scripture Meditation:

"For the word of God is alive and active. Sharper than any double-edged sword ..."—Hebrews 4:1

Queen's Challenge:

Buy a dedicated notebook—your own *Notebook of Heaven*. Start today.

1. Choose one verse. (You can start with Psalms, Proverbs, or the Gospels.)
2. Write it out by hand.
3. Below the verse, write:

    ♛   What does it reveal about God?

    _____

    _____

    _____

    _____

_____

_____

♛   What does it reveal about you?

_____

_____

_____

_____

_____

_____

♛   How does it challenge or comfort you?

_____

_____

_____

_____

_____

_____

♛   Think of a short prayer in response.

_____

_____

_____

_____

_____

_____

Prayer:

"God, let Your Word root itself in me. Let every lie fall under the weight of Your truth. Train me in righteousness. Transform me in silence. Let me hunger for You more than I hunger for anything this world can offer."

How does the scripture speak to your heart?

_____

_____

_____

_____

_____

_____

_____

_____

_____

_____

_____

_____

_____

_____

_____

_____

_____

_____

Chapter 6

Deliverance in the Secret Place

Deliverance is not a public event.

It is not an Instagram post, not a viral moment, not a conference altar call for applause. It is personal, private, and deeply spiritual. It happens in silence, in surrender, and in the kind of sacred space that no one else gets to enter—just you and God.

This chapter is not about what people saw—this is about what they didn't.

Because while the world celebrated my elevation, I was undergoing a divine excavation—a tearing down of old altars, identities, idols, lies, soul ties, and agreements I didn't even know I had made. Deliverance wasn't neat. It wasn't polished. It wasn't easy. It was a breaking of the chains. A confrontation. A detox. A holy collision between who I had become and who God always knew I was.

It began the moment I asked God a dangerous question:

"Show me what needs to go."

And He did.

He showed me people I needed to forgive.

He showed me relationships I had built on brokenness and trauma.

He revealed insecurities masquerading as confidence.

He exposed wounds I had tried to medicate with money, attention, control, and power.

I had spent years silencing my pain with performance. I learned how to look fine, act fine, and work fine. Yet underneath it all, I was bleeding, and God wasn't interested in decorating my cage—He came to break the lock.

Though before He delivered me, He had to show me what was, in truth, enslaving me.

That's what the secret place is. It's the place where the Holy Spirit sits you down, opens your eyes, and says, *This is what we're going to heal.* Not because He's cruel, but because He's a good Father. A holy surgeon. A God who doesn't just cleanse what's visible—He heals what's deep.

I remember one morning, after studying a passage in Psalms, I fell on my face and sobbed for hours. Not because of shame—but because the presence of God was so near, and for the first time, I knew I was safe enough to fall apart.

Real deliverance will do that to you.

It will make you weep, not because you are condemned, but because you realize you've been carrying burdens you were never designed to carry. It will make you lay down the mask, the makeup, the business cards, the ambition—and finally come to Him as a daughter.

That's where I met Him. Not at the front of a room, but in my office. On the floor. In sweatpants. No music. No makeup. Just me—raw and wrecked.

And do you know what He said?

Not, *"You should've known better."*

Not, *"You're too late."*

He said, *"I've been waiting for you."*

The secret place became my sanctuary. My soul's recovery room. It became holy ground because I chose to meet Him there—again and again and again.

Deliverance is a process. Sometimes God removes things instantly. Other times, He peels them off layer by layer, moment by moment. Some days, I felt powerful. Other days, I felt exposed. Yet every day I felt His presence, and in His presence, there is freedom.

Freedom from addiction.

Freedom from idolatry.

Freedom from fear.

Freedom from shame.

Freedom from the counterfeit version of yourself you've been forced to live in barely to survive.

To the woman reading this who is still performing, still pretending, still dressing up your pain—I want to tell you that the secret place is not a punishment.

It is a **gift**. An invitation. An open door to healing that won't embarrass you but empower you.

You don't need to be strong in the secret place. You need to be *honest*.

You don't need to perform. You need to surrender.

You don't need to shout. You need to whisper, "*Help me.*"

And He will—every hidden wound, every hidden fear, every whispered lie that says you'll never be whole.

He will address it. He will confront it. Then, ***He will deliver you***.

You will rise up differently. Not immediately perfect, but undeniably changed.

Because once you've been in the presence of the Deliverer, nothing else satisfies. Not platforms. Not titles. Not praise.

Just Him.

Scripture Meditation:

"He who dwells in the secret place of the Most High shall abide under the shadow of the Almighty."—Psalm 91:1

Queen's Challenge:

Set aside thirty minutes this week for uninterrupted, undistracted time in the secret place. Go into a room, close the door, and sit with God.

Ask Him:

♔ What lies am I still believing about myself?

_____

_____

_____

_____

_____

_____

♔ What am I still holding on to that You want to heal?

_____

_____

_____

_____

_____

_____

♔ Where am I still performing instead of abiding?

_____

_____

_____

_____

_____

_____

Write down what He shows you. Don't rush the moment. Be still. Let Him speak.

Prayer:

"Father, deliver me in the places no one sees. Heal the wounds I've hidden. Reveal the chains I've carried. I surrender every mask, every idol, every pain. Make me whole in Your presence. In Jesus' name, Amen."

How does the scripture speak to your heart?

_____

_____

_____

_____

_____

_____

_____

_____

_____

_____

_____

_____

_____

_____

_____

_____

NIGHTLIFE QUEEN TO KINGDOM QUEEN

Chapter 7

The Word That Found Me

There are moments in your life when time slows down—when Heaven steps into your story and what you've whispered in private is shouted back at you in power. You cannot manufacture these moments. You cannot script them. They are holy. Yet once they happen, you will never forget them.

This was mine.

It was a Sunday at 10:27 a.m., and I wasn't even at my home church. I attended services at my friend Sasha's church. A prophet was there, Chris Beleke. I had walked into the sanctuary expecting nothing but maybe a word of encouragement, a sermon to chew on, but God had planned an encounter. One that would become a divine marker in my story. *John 10:27 states: "My sheep hear my voice, and I know them, and they follow me."*

Worship had just ended. The presence of God was already heavy in the room, like thick oil in the air. Sasha pushed our way through to the altar to receive prayer. There we stood quietly, heads bowed, eyes closed. I watched as those around us were prayed over while we were quietly passed by. When I looked up, it was just the two of us in front of the church. A church I had never been to before. Then, I heard the prophet begin to speak.

I didn't know him. He didn't know me. Even so, he began calling out a woman—*me*.

He began with, "God has a word for you."

"I hear Kourtney ... Kourtney."

I wept uncontrollably at this point. He was repeating prayers I had only ever spoken alone in my time with God. He voiced things I had journaled but never shared.

He echoed the cries of my heart that I hadn't even had the language to articulate fully. Every word pierced not just my emotions, but my spirit.

He said, "You've been crying out to him. You've laid down what others thought was a crown, and God says, 'Because you've chosen Me in secret, I will honor you in the open.' You are stepping into a new assignment—that everything your heart desires is on this side. Are you ready to sacrifice what you think you love?"

He said, "I see Martini Bar."

I broke—not in embarrassment, but in confirmation.

I knew in that moment ... God had been listening.

Every late-night prayer.
Every whispered, "God, I'm trying."
Every journaled scripture.
Every act of obedience when no one was watching.
He had seen it all, and now, He was answering publicly what I had prayed for privately.

This wasn't a generic prophecy. It was surgical. Divine. Unmistakable.

I want to pause and say this: If you've ever wondered whether God sees you, hears you, or even *remembers* you—He does, and when He confirms it, He often does it through others.

The Word I received that day wasn't just affirmation. It was *instruction*. A declaration of who I genuinely was. It called me higher. It called me out. It called me forward.

I took that Word and wrote it down. I meditated on it. I warred with it. Because prophecy is not just encouragement—it's a sword you are destined to wield. It's a promise wrapped in a process, and your agreement is required.

I began to walk differently after that day. Not because the Word made me proud, but because it made me accountable. When Heaven confirms your calling, it also begins refining your character. I couldn't go back to old places. Couldn't entertain old conversations. Couldn't dress wounds that God had already begun to heal.

I had been marked. I had been seen. And now, I had been sent.

That Word carried me through some of the most difficult spiritual battles I would face in the months that followed because after a prophecy comes warfare. The enemy consistently attacks what has been affirmed by Heaven. I now had proof that God had spoken, and that proof became my anchor.

To the woman reading this: If you have received a Word—whether from a prophet, a sermon, a dream, or a whisper in prayer—steward it.

Write it down. Test it against the Word of God. Pray into it. Let it shape you. Let it guide your decisions. Let it challenge your comfort.

Because God doesn't give you a Word to entertain you—He gives you a Word to transform you.

Perhaps you haven't received a prophetic Word yet, and that's okay.

Start with the written Word. God has already spoken over you:

- ♛ You are chosen.

- ♛ You are fearfully and wonderfully made.

- ♛ You are not abandoned.

- ♛ You are called for such a time as this.

So when the time comes, if God chooses to send confirmation through a messenger, you will know. Because His sheep know His voice, and when He speaks, your soul will respond.

I left that church that day a completely different person—a new creature in Christ Jesus.

Not because a man made me feel good, but because God had confirmed what He had already been whispering.

It was then I knew—I was walking into my next chapter. I was not just recovering. I was being *recommissioned*.

Scripture Meditation:

"Believe in the Lord your God, so shall you be established; believe His prophets, so shall you prosper."—2 Chronicles 20:20

Queen's Challenge:

Have you received a Word from God—through prophecy, prayer, or scripture?

    ♛   Write it down.

_____

_____

_____

_____

_____

    ♛   Ask: What instructions come with it?

_____

_____

_____

_____

_____

    ♛   Are you obeying it? Or are you waiting for it to come true without moving?

_____

_____

_____

_____

_____

_____

If you've never received a prophetic word, open the Word of God and begin to underline every promise that applies to you. Speak them aloud. Let God confirm His truth in your spirit.

Prayer:

"God, thank You for speaking. Whether through Your Word or Your servants, I choose to listen. Help me steward every promise You've declared over my life. Make me sensitive to Your voice. Please give me the courage to walk in the calling You've confirmed. In Jesus' name, Amen."

How does the scripture speak to your heart?

_____

_____

_____

_____

_____

_____

_____

_____

_____

_____

_____

_____

_____

_____

Chapter 8

Beauty for Ashes

There is a kind of letting go that feels like dying.

The unraveling of a life you built with your own hands. The release of the identity you fought to maintain. The decision to walk away from what once made you feel powerful, important, and seen.

It's not glamorous by any stretch of imagination. It's not always praised. Yet, it's the most sacred kind of surrender there is—because it's the moment when you choose God's will over your own. It's that moment where you begin to understand the true meaning of Free Will.

This was the season when I laid it all down.

Lit Cigar & Martini Lounge—my baby, my brand, my crown jewel—no longer held the same place in my heart. I could feel the shift. What used to thrill me now felt hollow. What once made me proud now felt burdensome. I knew: this part of my life had reached its divine expiration date.

Obedience required *release*, and if I'm honest, it terrified me.

I worked so hard. Pushed through adversity. Built an empire from vision and grit. I had achieved everything the world said would make me whole, and now God was saying, *Let it go.*

Not because He wanted to punish me, but because He wanted to FREE ME.

I wish I could say I walked away smiling, but I didn't. There were tears. Fears. Questions. Doubts. Would I still be significant without the title? Would I still be respected without the brand? Who was I outside of what I had built?

Like a tide, something in my spirit had shifted too profoundly for me to stay. I had been called out of *Egypt.*

At last, when God calls you out, you must choose: the familiarity of bondage or the uncertainty of freedom.

So I walked. It was time to carry my cross and be on my way. One step at a time. Out of the club. Out of the brand. Out of the identity I had created without Him.

I walked out of what made sense, into what made faith. I walked away from applause, into silence. I walked away from the known, into the Kingdom.

Suddenly, what happened next?

Ashes.

Grief over what was. Loneliness from people who didn't understand. Whispers from those who mocked what they couldn't comprehend.

But also—*beauty*.

Peace that surpassed every dollar I had ever made. Clarity about who I truly was. A relationship with God that didn't just visit on Sundays but walked with me daily.

Provision that came without pressure. Doors that opened without manipulation. Opportunities that aligned with purpose, not performance.

Most of all, the kind of joy that doesn't come from circumstance—it comes from presence.

I want to speak to the woman reading this—standing at her crossroads:
You know something has to be laid down.
You feel the nudge.
The call.
The whisper.
Yet fear grips you because what if obedience leads to loss?

Let me tell you: obedience **does** lead to loss—but only of what was never meant to keep you.

Everything I laid down, God replaced.
Every crown I surrendered, He exchanged.
Every false identity I released, He redefined.

However, the ashes had to come first.

We love the word "beauty," but we forget that in Isaiah 61:3, it says *beauty for ashes*.
Not *instead of*, but *in exchange for*.

That means something must burn.

Not out of cruelty—out of love.

Because God will never allow you to keep something that competes with Him. He is a consuming fire—not because He wants to destroy you, but because He wants to **refine you**.

If you are in a season where things are falling apart, ask yourself:

    ♔   Is this God tearing down what I built without Him?

    ♔   Is this God inviting me to build again—but this time, on His foundation?

Don't fight the fire. Let burn what cannot stay because on the other side of ashes, there is always *beauty*.

Not the kind the world gives, but the kind only God can provide.

He gave me laughter again. He gave me rest. He gave me dreams I hadn't dared to speak aloud. He gave me divine friendships.

He gave me a vision that didn't stress me, but blessed me. He gave me a crown that *no one could take away*—because it was placed by **His** hand, not man's.

This is the divine exchange. This is the gift of surrender. This is the *glory after the fire*.

Scripture Meditation:

"To all who mourn ... He will give a crown of beauty for ashes, a joyous blessing instead of mourning, festive praise instead of despair."
—Isaiah 61:3

Queen's Challenge:

Take a moment today and ask God:

♛ What am I holding onto that You want to replace?

  _____

  _____

  _____

  _____

  _____

  _____

♛ What ashes am I afraid to surrender?

  _____

  _____

  _____

  _____

  _____

  _____

♛ What am I grieving that You've already called me out of?

  _____

  _____

  _____

  _____

  _____

  _____

Then write it down. Lay it before Him in prayer.

Prayer:

"Father, I give You my ashes. Every dream, title, relationship, and identity that I've clung to—I surrender. I trust You to give me beauty, not just in return, but because it's who You are. Let Your fire refine me, not destroy me. Let me rise from the ashes clothed in glory. In Jesus' name, men."

How does the scripture speak to your heart?

_____

_____

_____

_____

_____

_____

_____

_____

_____

_____

_____

_____

_____

Chapter 9

The Other Side of Obedience

There is a sacred tension between *promise* and *fulfillment*—a space that feels like both wilderness and holy ground. It's the space between hearing God speak and watching Him move. Between the Word given and the Word fulfilled.

That space is called obedience—and most people never make it across.

They hear the prophecy. They feel the conviction. They even start the journey. Yet when obedience begins to cost them comfort, familiarity, relationships, and influence, t hey stop. They look back at Egypt. They miss the leeks and onions. They forget about the slavery.

If you want to walk in Kingdom destiny, you have to walk through the narrow gate that few choose: radical obedience.

For me, that gate looked like walking away from everything I built with my own hands and trusting God to build something better with His.

After the prophecy, after the letting go, after the surrender, I began to obey—not just in the big, dramatic ways, but in the daily, unseen choices.

I chose stillness over strategy, prayer over performance, studying over scrolling.

Where I once bent to people-pleasing, I began to build boundaries—and honor them.

I chose obedience even when it made no sense—and especially when it hurt. What I discovered surprised me: obedience isn't glamorous, but it's the bridge between bondage and breakthrough where *everything shifts.*

As I walked in obedience, I started seeing the Word that had been spoken over me come to life—piece by piece, promise by promise. Opportunities began opening that I didn't chase. Provision came in ways I didn't orchestrate.

People entered my life who didn't just affirm me—they *aligned* with God's purpose for me.

My creativity flourished again—not for fame, but for impact. Most of all, I had peace—not the kind of peace that comes from things going right, but a peace that comes from being rightly positioned inside His will. You'll learn quickly: obedience positions you for divine provision.

Let me say that again: obedience positions you for divine provision.

The favor you're praying for is often waiting on the other side of a decision you're afraid to make.

We love declarations. We love worship. We love the idea of faith, but faith without obedience is fantasy. You cannot declare your way into purpose while *disobeying your way out of alignment.*

God is merciful, yes, but He is also precise. His promises are often tied to conditions. His blessings flow through alignment, not ambition.

Think of Abraham.
Think of Moses.
Think of Esther.
Think of Mary.
Think of Jesus.

Every breakthrough in the Bible was followed by a moment of terrifying obedience. Every time someone said yes, God moved.

So, I kept saying yes, and God kept saying *move*. Even when I didn't feel ready. Even when my bank account didn't match the vision. Even when others questioned me. Even when the path ahead looked uncertain.

Remarkably, every time I obeyed, I felt Heaven respond. Obedience activated blessings I didn't even know were waiting.

It wasn't just about doing the right thing. It was about *becoming the right vessel*—the kind that Heaven could trust. The kind that could carry glory. That no longer chased platforms, but built altars.

I want to speak to you now, woman of God, who is standing on the edge of your yes: That instruction God gave you? That nudge you keep feeling? That thing you've been procrastinating out of fear?

That's the gate. Now walk through it. Don't wait for clarity to obey. Obey, and clarity will come.

Everything you're asking God for—peace, joy, identity, breakthrough, alignment—is not on the other side of performance. It's on the other side of obedience.

You don't have to do it perfectly. You only have to do it faithfully. One yes at a time. One act of obedience at a time.

Over time, you'll look back and realize that the narrow road led you to everything your soul ever longed for.

Not comfort, but calling. Not recognition, but revelation. Not applause, but authority.

Very soon, you'll realize that obedience didn't cost you anything worth keeping. It only took the burdens you were never meant to bear.

Scripture Meditation:

"If you are willing and obedient, you shall eat the good of the land."— Isaiah 1:19

Queen's Challenge:

What is the last thing God told you to do?

♚ Did you do it?

_____

_____

_____

_____

_____

_____

♚ Are you delaying?

_____

_____

_____

_____

_____

_____

♛ Are you compromising?

_____

_____

_____

_____

_____

_____

Write it down. Be honest.

Prayer:

"Lord, I want to walk in complete obedience. Not delayed, not partial—full obedience. Give me the courage to do what You've called me to do, even when it costs. I trust You with the outcome. I trust You with my name. I trust You with my future. In Jesus' name, Amen."

Then, take the step. Do the thing. Say the no. Make the call. Shut the door. Open your hands.

Everything you're praying for is waiting on the other side of your yes.

How does the scripture speak to your heart?

_____

_____

_____

_____

_____

_____

_____

_____

_____

_____

_____

_____

_____

_____

_____

_____

_____

_____

_____

_____

Chapter 10

Queen Reborn

There is a point in every transformation story when the ashes settle, the storm quiets, and the mirror no longer reflects a survivor—but a woman *reborn*.

This is that moment.

After the obedience.
After the release.
After the tearing down.
After the prophecy.
After the silence and secret surrender.
God didn't just deliver me. He *reintroduced me* … to myself.

I looked in the mirror and saw a woman I had never truly known:
Peaceful.
Powerful.
Whole.
Royal.

Not because of status. Not because of achievement, but because I had been *reconciled with my original design*.

The girl who once performed for applause now stood rooted in identity.
The woman who once built her name was now content bearing **His**.
The queen of nightlife had become a queen of the **Kingdom**.

I need you to understand something deeply spiritual about that transformation: God didn't rescue me *to fix me*. He rescued me to *restore me to the throne He had ordained before the foundations of the world.*

A throne not of diamonds and spotlight—but of *purpose, wisdom, fire,* and *spiritual authority.*

Because when God calls you queen, He is not speaking to your persona. He is speaking to your *position*—a position that predates your trauma. Predates your titles. Predates your failures.

You were always chosen. You were always marked. You were always more than what you settled for.

The rebirth didn't happen in a moment. It was slow. Layered. Deep. Yet it was real.

God started giving me vision again—this time not for image or entertainment, but for *impact.*

He began giving me assignments that aligned with Heaven. Conversations that stirred the anointing. Relationships that were divine in their timing and intention. I wasn't just living—I was *reigning*. In peace. In clarity. In truth.

No longer building altars to the world, but now building **Kingdom legacies**.

I felt powerful, but not in the way I once chased. This power was *quiet, humble,* and *authoritative* because it was anchored in submission

. My voice carried weight—not because it was loud, but because it was *His*.

I've become the woman I was always destined to be—and beloved, so will you.

You were never designed to compete with the world. You were called to *transform it*.

You were never supposed to strive for worth. God crowned you *at creation*.

The Kingdom Queen does not perform. She abides. She does not rule through control. She rules through *wisdom*. She does not need validation—she walks in *revelation*.

She does not fear the fire—because she's already been through it and survived.

This is the rise of the *reborn woman*. She is dangerous to darkness because she knows her God.

She prays with authority. She lives with purpose. She forgives with freedom. She speaks with fire. Most importantly, she worships with everything she has because she remembers where God found her.

If you're still wondering if that can be your story too—*it already is*.

If you've come this far in this book, it's not by accident. It's your invitation to stand. To rise. To take your place in the Kingdom—not as a polished woman with all the answers, but as a daughter of the Most High who is ready to reign in truth.

Your rebirth won't look like mine.

Yet it will bear the same fruit:

- ♛ Peace that the world cannot give

- ♛ Joy that doesn't waver with circumstances

- ♛ Discernment that pierces through lies

- ♛ Authority rooted in humility

- ♛ Fire that cannot be extinguished

One day soon, you'll look in the mirror and realize something: *you're not who you used to be.* You've been born again-not just into faith, but into *identity.* You'll no longer apologize for your voice, your calling, your past, or your power.

Your crown doesn't come from culture—it comes from **Christ**.

And when Heaven crowns you queen, nothing and no one can take it away.

Scripture Meditation:

"But you are a chosen people, a royal priesthood, a holy nation, God's special possession ..."—1 Peter 2:9

Queen's Challenge:

Look in the mirror. Literally. Today.

Say aloud:

"I am royalty. I am chosen. I am a daughter of the King. I reign in righteousness. I rule in truth. I walk in purpose. I carry peace. I am not going back."

Then write your own "Rebirth Declaration"—a one-page affirmation of who you are in Christ.

Begin it with *"The old me is gone. The new me is crowned."*

_____

_____

_____

_____

_____

_____

_____

_____

_____

_____

_____

Prayer:

"Father, thank You for making me new. Thank You for rewriting my story, for crowning me in places I thought I'd die in, for redeeming every broken chapter. I declare today that I am not returning to the former things. I walk in my Kingdom identity. I will take my place. I am Yours, and You are mine. In Jesus' name, Amen."

How does the scripture speak to your heart?

_____

_____

_____

_____

_____

_____

_____

_____

_____

_____

_____

_____

_____

_____

_____

_____

_____

_____

_____

_____

_____

_____

Epilogue

To the Queen Still in the Dark

To the woman reading this who feels like she's drowning in her own silence …
To the one who shows up strong but cries herself to sleep …
To the one with lashes and labels, but a spirit that's breaking …

This is for you.

I see you—because *I was you.*

You're standing in a room full of people and still feel invisible.
You're praised for your beauty but starving for truth.
You're giving your all to everyone else but can't remember the last time you felt whole.
You've mastered the art of showing up while quietly fading inside.
You've built a life they all want, but deep down you're wondering, *Is this all there is?*

There's a version of you that the world celebrates. However, there's a version of you that only Heaven knows—a woman the enemy has fought hard to keep buried beneath performance, trauma, applause, addiction, fear, and disappointment.

Let me tell you a secret the devil never wanted you to know:
The real you is still in there. She exists.
The royal you. She exists.
The whole you. She exists.
The anointed you. She exists.
The dangerous-as-hell you. She exists more than ever now.

Just know God is not waiting for you to fix everything before He calls you. He is calling you *now*: in the midst of your contradictions, in the middle of your confusion, in the silence after your sin.

He's not intimidated by your history.
He's not shocked by your habits.
He's not offended by your questions.

He is just waiting for your **yes**.

Not your perfect yes.
Not your polished yes.
Just your surrendered one.

It will be in that moment—when you finally whisper, "*God, I'm tired*"—that Heaven begins to move.

I want to tell you:
There *is* life after the dark.
There *is* joy after the betrayal.
There *is* power after the performance.
There *is* purpose after the wilderness.
There *is* love that doesn't leave.
There *is* a throne—but it's not in the club. It's not on Instagram. It's not in the applause.

It's in the **Kingdom**, and it was made for **YOU**.

I know you might not believe it yet. That's okay. I'll believe it for you until you can. I'll stand on this side of healing and whisper across the divide, *"It's real. He's real. You're not too far gone. Come home."*

You don't have to die in the identity you created for survival. You can rise into the one you were born to carry.

You are not disqualified. You are not disowned. You are not discredited.

You are **called**. You are **chosen**. You are **crowned**.

So, Queen, if you're still in the dark … breathe. Lift your head. Close your eyes.

Say the name that saved me: **"Jesus."** He will come. Not because you earned it, but because you're His.

The Kingdom has room for you. The throne is waiting, and so am I.

Welcome home.

> **Scripture Meditation:**
>
> *"The people who walked in darkness have seen a great light; those who dwelt in the land of deep darkness, on them has light shone."*— Isaiah 9:2

Final Queen's Challenge:

Wherever you are on your journey—start today.

One whisper. One prayer. One honest sentence to God.

Write it down. Say it aloud. Believe it anyway.

_____

_____

_____

_____

_____

_____

_____

_____

_____

_____

_____

_____

_____

_____

_____

_____

_____

_____

Then watch as everything begins to change—because the light you've been longing for?

You were born to walk in it. You're a *Kingdom Queen*.

How does the scripture speak to your heart?

_____

_____

_____

_____

_____

_____

_____

_____

_____

_____

_____

_____

_____

_____

_____

_____

_____

_____

_____

_____

_____

_____

_____

www.ingramcontent.com/pod-product-compliance
Lightning Source LLC
Chambersburg PA
CBHW051229120626
46547CB00013B/1570